SOUTH AFRICA
from the air

HERMAN POTGIETER
SOUTH AFRICA
from the air

ACKNOWLEDGEMENTS

I am deeply indebted to the following organizations and pilots for their help in creating the images for this book: •Nitani Air: Chris Briers, Ferdie Kahts and Johnny Navarro; •Lansav: Kuno von Dürkheim and Rob Sproul; •Buzzair: Buzz Bezuidenhout; •Midwest Aviation: Les Daly; •NAC: Neil Southey; •Court Helicopters: Sue Beatty, Clive Bartmann, Roger Watt and Ken Whittal; •Heliquip: Zack Zunckel; •Anglo American Properties Ltd; •The Conservation Corporation and Phinda; and •Mercedes Benz South Africa Ltd. Also Ola Grinaker; Sean Lindsey; Johan Swart and Anton Verwey of the University of Stellenbosch Flying Club; Paddy Carolan; Ed Goetsch and Basil Newham; and Don Pigott of FEDICS.
Gentlemen and lady, my sincere thanks to you, and to all those others who were involved in one way or another.

My photographic equipment comprised Nikon F3 and F4 cameras fitted variously with 35, 58, 85 and 105 mm Nikkor lenses, though on the odd occasion I also used Pentax 645 and Linhoff 617 cameras. Film stock was Fujichrome RF50, RVP50 and RDP100.

DEDICATION
For my mother Pauline, and for Jackie and Paul

Struik Publishers
(a member of The Struik Group (Pty) Ltd)
80 McKenzie Street, Cape Town 8001

Reg. No. 63/00203/07

First published 1992

Text ©Peter Joyce 1992
Photographs © Herman Potgieter 1992
Editor: Hilda Hermann
Designer: Abdul Amien
Cartographer: Angus Carr
Typesetting: Struik DTP
Reproduction: Unifoto (Pty) Ltd, Cape Town

Printed and bound by Tien Wah Press (Pte) Ltd, Singapore

ISBN 1 86825 285 X

CONTENTS

Introduction
6

TRANSVAAL
10

ORANGE FREE STATE
46

NATAL
56

CAPE PROVINCE
94

Index
160

t is around the Cape of Good Hope that the *Flying Dutchman*, that phantom ship with broken masts, tattered sheets and a tormented ghost of a captain, is destined to sail until Doomsday. A fanciful legend, perhaps, but one cherished by generations of seafarers, and given eerie substance by the many 'sightings' recorded, including one by the future King George V, while he was serving as a Royal Navy midshipman. The seas here, beneath the awesome bulk of Cape Point, are cold, turbulent, hostile, swept by blustery, south-easterly winds that often turn into gales of fearsome proportions.

Far away, close to the sluggish, tropically warm waters of the Limpopo River, is Messina, a modest town distinguished chiefly by the giant, grotesquely shaped baobabs – the 'upside-down trees' of African lore – in its encircling nature reserve. The rocks of the area are unusual too: formed nearly 4 000 million ago, they are among the earth's most ancient geological formations.

Both Cape Point and Messina, 2 000 kilometres apart and belonging, it seems, to different worlds, are part of South Africa: the former is at the country's southern extremity, the latter at its northern.

South Africa is a big country: 1 220 430 square kilometres in extent, which is five times larger than the British Isles, or roughly the size of France, Germany, Italy and Holland combined. It encloses within its borders the independent kingdoms of Lesotho and Swaziland, shares its northern frontiers with the desert republic of Namibia, with Botswana, Zimbabwe and Mozambique. To the east and south are the warm waters of the Indian Ocean; to the west the chilly Atlantic – a long coastline, almost 3 000 kilometres in all, that is remarkably regular: there are few pronounced embayments or natural harbours.

A bird's-eye perspective of this vast land would reveal a clear, quite simple topographical pattern. There are two distinct physical regions: the great interior plateau, varying in height from the relatively low 600 m of the Kalahari basin to the lofty, 3 400-m Maluti Mountains in the east, occupies most of the subcontinent; and, secondly, the narrow coastal zone, which fringes the plateau on three sides. Between the two is the Great Escarpment, an almost continuous chain of mountain ranges of which the Drakensberg, in Natal, is the highest and most spectacular. Within this fairly straightforward configuration, though, there is immense diversity – of climate and scenery, rock, soil and vegetation, in addition to ethnic character. Climatically, South Africa could be half a dozen entirely separate countries. The eastern seaboard, for instance, is warm, wet, lushly subtropical, while some parts of the western maritime region get no more than 50 millimetres of rain a year and the terrain is a wilderness of sand and stunted plant.

And because climatic and other conditions vary so dramatically from area to area, the country's farmers are able to produce just about every major crop and a good number of minor ones, among them maize, which takes up about half the arable lands; wheat, grain, sorghum, sunflower seed, tobacco, cotton, citrus, sugarcane, deciduous fruits – and grapes, both for export purposes and for the south-

Boksburg's suburbia encroaches ever farther into the farmlands of the East Rand (*opposite*). The community draws its prosperity from the gold and coal of the area; early residents had the foresight to beautify what could have been just another dusty mining town, and Boksburg now ranks as one of the Transvaal's more attractive urban centres.

The high-rise elegance of modern Durban (*left*).

western Cape's magnificent wine industry. All this despite the generally poor quality of the soils (only 12 percent of the land area can be cultivated) and the generally low rainfall (the mean annual figure is just half the global average). Huge expanses are also given over to livestock; the national wool clip is the world's fourth largest.

There is diversity, too, in what lies beneath the earth. South Africa has more than twenty distinct geological regions, which accounts for the broad spectrum of its mineral resources. The ancient Swazian and Randian formations of the highveld yield vast quantities of gold; iron and manganese are mined in the western Transvaal; platinum and chrome in the central Transvaal; coal in the Karoo Sequence (reserves are estimated at 60 billion tons); diamonds in the kimberlite pipes of the northern Cape; copper, zinc, uranium, cobalt, nickel, phosphates – the list runs to nearly 60 commodities.

The agricultural bounty and the minerals are the base ingredients of a sophisticated national economy, one which employs modern technologies, advanced communications, highly developed commercial and banking sectors. In short, South Africa is a continental superpower: among other things it accounts for 40 percent of Africa's industrial output and manufactured exports, 70 percent of its generated electricity, 75 percent of its railed goods, 46 percent of its motor vehicles, 36 percent of its telephones.

All in all, an impressive catalogue of assets. But the figures are relative, and deceptive: South Africa is a developing country and properly belongs in the Third rather than the First World; its gross domestic product is less than that of Belgium, and not much greater than that of the tiny American state of Maryland – which are sobering facts indeed.

South Africa has a kaleidoscopic population of close on 40 million, by far the largest portion comprising black people belonging to many different language and cultural

● WINDHOEK

NAMIBIA

RICHTERSVELD

NAMAQUAL
● Springbok

ATLANTIC OCEAN

Lamberts Bay ●

Paternoster ●

Saldanha Bay ●
**WEST COAST
NATIONAL PARK**

Stellenbos
CAPE TOWN ●
Gordons Ba

The Indian Ocean surf pounds the rocks on the seaward side of Durban's Bluff (*right*). The bay, enclosed by the two arms of Bluff and Point, is one of the few natural harbours along South Africa's coast.

groupings, though the distinctions are fast disappearing as urban drift – mass migration to the cities – erodes the values, the traditions, the character of old Africa. Numerically much smaller components of South African society are its 900 000 Indians, most of whom live in Natal; its mixed-decent ('Coloured') community, three million strong and concentrated in the south-western Cape; and some five million whites of varied European ancestry. These peoples were, until recently, kept apart by law, regulation and by corrosive prejudice, but the country is in rapid transition and today, after decades of rigid segregation, they are coming together to create a new South Africa. If their efforts succeed – and given a modicum of peace, stability and faith, they must – this most beautiful and complex of countries will become the jewel of Africa.

Transvaal

The jacaranda-garlanded elegance of a Johannesburg colonial-style property (*previous page*). The more opulent of these houses originally belonged to the enormously wealthy Randlords of the city's golden era, flamboyant public figures who nevertheless sought residential privacy, building secluded and luxurious homes 'with skylights and turrets, scrolled verandahs and gild-ed tips to their fences'. Many such mansions were to be found in the northern suburb of Parktown, including Dolobran, pictured, which was completed in 1905.

Hillbrow (*right*), one of Johannesburg's inner suburbs, is reported to be the most densely populated urban area in the southern hemisphere. It is a bustling, cosmopolitan, high-rise flatland of tall and crowded tenements, speciality shops, eateries, discos and streets that seldom sleep. The J.G. Strijdom tower stands some 269 m high and is among the most prominent of the city's landmarks.

Thousands gather in Johannesburg's Ellis Park stadium for a charity concert (*opposite*). Local music is distinctive, a mixture that draws variously from early township jazz, the big American bands of the 1930s, the rural 'mbubi' choral groups, the joyous penny-whistle lilt of long-gone Sophiatown, the soul-sounds of the 1970s and the Afro-rock of the '80s. It all comes together under the somewhat loose heading of 'mbaqanga', which is the name given to African maize bread and which, like the food it describes, fills a deep need.

TRANSVAAL

he Witwatersrand – the 'ridge of white waters' that rises above the flattish, dun-coloured Transvaal highveld – is a modest enough physical feature, barely deserving of its rather grand name. But it does form a major watershed and, much more important in terms of both history and economics, it is the repository of a golden lode that, on its discovery a little over a century ago, attracted thousands of fortune-seekers. They came from all quarters of the globe, and their first encampment – a dusty, fly-blown sprawl of tents, rudimentary shacks and canteens – grew up to become known as modern Johannesburg.

Pretoria, 60 kilometres to the north, is the Transvaal's – and South Africa's – capital city, but Johannesburg ranks as the country's largest metropolis, financial hub of the subcontinent and the epicentre of a vast muddle of independent mining, industrial and dormitory towns collectively named after the ridge. To the south, around the broad middle reaches of the Vaal river, is another heavily populated area, a smoke-hazed urban patchwork that embraces the so-called Vaal Triangle. Taken together, Pretoria, the Witwatersrand and the Vaal Triangle – the PWV area for short – occupies just two percent of South Africa's land surface but accommodates a quarter of the country's population and generates nearly 50 percent of the national income. It's an immensely affluent region (though there is massive poverty here as well) which still receives its impetus and draws much of its wealth from the gold mines. Today, however, the economic spectrum comprises a great deal more.

The Transvaal is an economic giant, the Rhur of Africa. But the province is also blessed with scenic richness, even splendour in parts, and its wildlife heritage is incomparable. The gently undulating Highveld plains east of the Witwatersrand gradually give way to outcrops and hills, and then to mountains that sweep up in a grandly imposing ridge. This is the northern segment of South Africa's Great Escarpment, here known as the Transvaal Drakensberg, a magnificent rampart of massif and verdant valley that stretches 300 kilometres from the town of Nelspruit northwards to Tzaneen and the misty, magical Magoebaskloof. Beyond the 'Berg, sprawling over the sun-blistered bushveld of the Lowveld plain, is the Kruger National Park, South Africa's premier game sanctuary.

Parktown (*left*), two kilometres north of central Johannesburg, was the pride of the early town planners: it was the first suburb built for the convenience and comfort of the richer settlers rather than for profit. Most of the early Randlords lived here, though little of the past now remains. One of the few palatial homes still standing is Sunnyside, once Lord Milner's residence and now an elegant private hotel.

Joubert Park (*above right*), one of the central area's few open spaces, was laid out in 1897, just a year after the first diggers erected their tents. It now features lawns, a plant conservatory, a floral clock, a giant open-air chessboard, and the Johannesburg Art Gallery, which contains among its wealth of exhibits some fine paintings, ceramics, textiles, and furniture.

Johannesburg is the financial heart of South Africa, a dynamic, ruggedly materialistic city at the epicentre of a vast complex of mining, industrial and dormitory towns collectively known as the Witwatersrand. A great deal of money is made, and sometimes lost, in the corridors of the central business district, huge new developments are launched almost by the month, and the skyline is ever-changing. Diagonal Street (*right*) features the distinctive Times Media building, and serves as the home of the Johannesburg Stock Exchange – one of the southern hemisphere's biggest and busiest financial markets.

The Village Walk (*opposite top*), one of Sandton's upmarket and imaginatively conceived shopping malls. Sandton, an independent municipality to the north of Johannesburg, is a relatively new town (it was founded in 1969) of fashionable suburbs and an unusual number of open green spaces. Its commercial centre, Sandton City, is one of the southern hemisphere's most sophisticated retail and business complexes.

Cluster-housing in the independent municipality of Randburg, just to the north of Johannesburg (*opposite lower*). In the early 1990s the national housing shortage amounted to something over a million units, though there was a surplus at the more affluent end of the market. Even among the relatively well off, however, the trend is towards the smaller home and higher-density development, for reasons of both economy and security.

Parkview golf course, Johannesburg (*left*). The central area is lamentably short of open ground, but there is plenty of suburban greenery; in all, the city council administers a healthy 600-plus parks and open spaces. The northern reaches have a splendid 'green lung' known as the Braamfontein Spruit, a stream that runs for about 25 km from Westdene dam to the Klein Jukskei river. Walkers can follow the spruit's park-like course for its full length virtually without touching concrete.

Formula I power-boat racing on the Rynfield dam, near the East Rand town of Benoni (*right*). The sport has a very keen following; with local competition being both fierce and skilled. Benoni (the biblical name means 'son of my sorrows', echoing an early surveyor's frustrations with the area) is one of the larger and more pleasant towns of what, in visual terms, is a generally undistinguished region.

Part of the Gold Reef City complex (*above*), an evocative re-creation of pioneer Johannesburg established on the Crown Mines site south of the central area. Attractions include train and omnibus rides, museums, period restaurants and pubs, a Victorian funfair and replicas of, among other things, early shops, a newspaper office, stock exchange, theatre, brewery, cooperage, apothecary and Chinese laundry.

Bruma (*left*), in the Witwatersrand municipality of Bedfordview and billed by its promoters as a 'Mediterranean oasis', is an appealing collage of speciality stores, boutiques, restaurants, coffee shops, cobbled and flower-bedecked alleyways, boardwalks and boating berths clustered around the shore of a small man-made lake.

Between Johannesburg and Pretoria is Midrand, a rapidly expanding cluster of residential suburbs, modern office blocks and 'clean' industrial sites. Much of the development is taking place around the once-modest village of Halfway House; in the foreground are the BMW premises. Among the area's tourist attractions are the Transvaal Snake Park and at nearby Kyalami, the Grand Prix circuit and the South African National Equestrian Centre which, among other things, trains a bevy of lovely Lippizaner stallions.

21

The M1 motorway slices through an old mining area south of Johannesburg (*top*). Some of the dumps are being recycled, the tailings reprocessed to glean gold that proved too elusive for earlier and less efficient extraction techniques.

A windspout – a miniature tornado – sucks up the dusty earth of Grand Central Aerodrome (*far right*), near the nascent metropolis of Midrand, which lies between Johannesburg and Pretoria. This is wintertime, the dry season: the life-giving rains usually begin in early summer (November) and last about five months, until February or March. In good years, Johannesburg and its neighbours get more rain than England's Manchester does in a full twelve-month period.

Fields of golden sunflowers (*right*), an uncharacteristically Elysian part of the East Rand countryside. Much of the region has succumbed to industrial development; among the bigger urban centres are Heidelburg, Nigel, Springs, Boksburg, Benoni and the city of Germiston.

The giant ISCOR (Iron and Steel Corporation) steelworks at Vanderbijlpark, in the Vaal Triangle conurbation south of Johannesburg. The town was named after Hendrik van der Bijl, an early 20th-century pioneer of the steel and power-generating industries and a brilliant experimental scientist. He invented the first scrambling device for radio communication, defined the principle of the thermonic valve (on which modern sound and visual broadcasting is based), and developed shortwave wireless communication over long distances.

Verwoerdburg, a large residential town to the south-east of Pretoria, is a rapidly developing centre of modern buildings and splendid sporting amenities, among them the excellent Centurion Park provincial cricket ground. Pictured (*above*) is the Verwoerdburg City shopping complex, and its dam, whose fountain is a fantasia of 30 metre high water jets.

Alexandra (*right*), one of the more prominent townships that fringe Johannesburg. The area, a small but densely populated one, suffered sporadic outbursts of civil strife in the early 1990s, much of it provoked by politically inspired antagonism.

Alexandra residents queue patiently to board taxis (*left*). The mini-buses, nicknamed 'Zola Budds' and 'Mary Deckers', provide a quicker – sometimes too quick – alternative to crowded trains and conventional buses. The 'black taxi' industry is one of the greatest success stories of the country's informal economy, a sector that flourishes without the burden of official regulation and which accounts for around 30 percent of the national income.

The foundations of Pretoria's imposing Voortrekker monument (*above*) were laid in 1938, the centenary of the Great Trek – the mass exodus of Dutch-speaking families from the Cape. The main block, 40 m high and ringed by a *laager* of 64 granite ox-wagons, comprises a domed Hall of Heroes and a lower chamber. Within the latter is a cenotaph, so sited that a ray of sunshine falls on the inscription, *Ons Vir Jou, Suid-Afrika* ('Our All For You, South Africa') precisely at noon on 16 December each year, the anniversary of the Battle of Blood River.

P retoria's skyscraping Volk-
skas Bank building (*left*) is one of
many aggressively modern high-rises
that have changed the face of South
Africa's administrative capital over
the past few decades. The city,
though, retains much from a more
leisurely and more dignified past.

The darkly gleaming Reserve Bank
building (*below*) rises elegantly above
central Pretoria.

Church Square (*above*), the heart of Pretoria, is dominated by a splendid bronze statue by Anton van Wouw of Paul Kruger, President of the Boer Republic of the Transvaal from 1883 until 1900, and regarded as the father of Afrikanerdom. Prominent among the flanking edifices are the Old Raadsaal, or council chambers, completed in 1890 in French Renaissance style; the elegant Palace of Justice, and the former Reserve Bank building, designed by the architect Sir Herbert Baker.

The Union Buildings (*right*), on Meintjes Kop, overlooking the city of Pretoria, are another of Sir Herbert Baker's splendid designs. They were completed in 1913, and served as a model for the grander but no more pleasing seat of the Raj government in Delhi, India.

Ahalf-hour's drive east of the Johannesburg-Pretoria axis will bring you to Hartebeespoort dam, a favourite haunt of weekend leisure seekers from the concrete jungle. Here there are hotels, chalets, camp sites, picnic spots and, away from the crowds, tranquility and scenic beauty as well. It covers 12 km^2 of the western Transvaal countryside at the foot of the lovely Magaliesberg range of hills, and the waters are especially popular among yachtsmen, anglers and other water sport enthusiasts. The flanking nature reserve has an enclosed game camp.

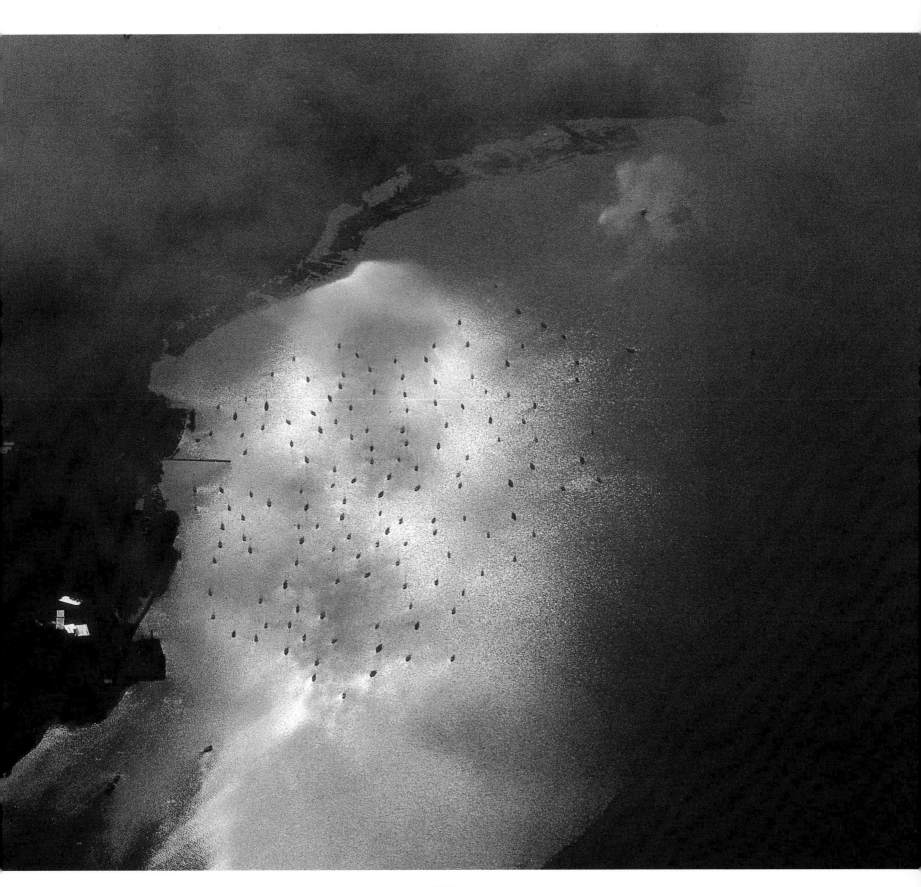

Low clouds wreathe the slopes of the Magaliesberg (*left*) to the west of Pretoria. The lovely range of hills extends 120 km to and just beyond the attractive and historic town of Rustenburg. The uplands are one of the last remaining havens of the stately Cape vulture.

The Rustenburg area of the western Transvaal (*above*) is blessed with some of the world's richest deposits of platinum-group metals; South African exports account for 42 per cent of global trade in these commodities. Rustenburg and its surrounds are scenically attractive, well watered, the countryside graced by the Magaliesberg and by farmlands rich with maize and wheat, tobacco, cotton, fruit and flowers.

The pretty little village of Kroondal, near Rustenburg in the western Transvaal. Founded on the farm Kronendal in 1843, the place was closely associated with the Hermannsburg Missionary Society, an early and influential German Lutheran organisation. Among the village school's alumni were Louis Botha, the Union of South Africa's first premier, and the Afrikaner poet J.D. du Toit, who wrote under the pen-name 'Totius'.

The small town of Mmabatho (*above*), administrative centre of Bophuthatswana. The region, deemed to be the 'homeland' of the Tswana and created in the 1970s and early 1980s as part of Pretoria's 'grand apartheid' strategy, comprises seven separate blocks of land scattered over three of South Africa's four provinces. Mmabatho, which means 'mother of the people', is in an area bordering the western Transvaal.

The Thaba N'chu Sun hotel-casino complex (*opposite top*), in the Orange Free State segment of Bophuthatswana. The town of Thaba N'chu ('black mountain') is noted for its charming church and for the beautiful hand-knitted Aran jerseys made locally.

Sun City (*right*), in the Bophuthatswana region to the north-west of Johannesburg, is one of the world's largest and most opulent resorts. The latest addition to the complex, flagship of Sun International, is the hugely ambitious 'Lost City' development and its ornate Palace Hotel.

40

The high Transvaal escarpment is renowned for its beautiful streams, cascades and waterfalls, many of them near the small forestry towns of Sabie and Graskop. The Mac-Mac falls (*opposite top*) plunge 58 m into a deep-green ravine dense with trees and ferns. A short distance away are the Mac-Mac pools, an exquisite setting for picnics and for communing with the gentler spirits.

This Ndebele showplace (*opposite*) gives some idea of traditional architecture and décor, though most authentic Ndebele dwellings have enclosed courtyards. Mural designs were originally simple geometrical patterns; later ones incorporated stylized representations of recognizable objects – plants and animals and, more recently, city scenes.

Among the many splendid scenic drives in the eastern Transvaal escarpment region is that over Robber's Pass (*left*), named after an especially inept early-1900s' highwayman. The road leads to Pilgrim's Rest, once a lively little 19th-century gold mining town and now a meticulously preserved 'living museum' that attracts tens of thousands of tourists each year.

The smoke-belching industries of Phalaborwa (*left*) set, rather incongruously, in the ruggedness of the Lowveld close to the borders of the Kruger National Park. The area has rich deposits of phosphates and other minerals; the town regularly records the country's highest temperatures.

Ebenezer dam (*above*), near Tzaneen in the magically beautiful northern segment of the Transvaal escarpment region, lies in the fertile Letaba river-valley. Other attractions in the area include the larger Fanie Botha dam, the New Agatha state forests, George's Valley and its vistas, and the magnificent Wolkberg Wilderness Area.

The clubhouse at Pietersburg (*top*), 'capital' of the far northern Transvaal and centre of a prosperous cattle-ranching region. The town is sited close to the Tropic of Capricorn but, because of its altitude (1 280 m), enjoys an equable climate.

Louis Trichardt (*above*), named after a leading Boer trekker of the mid-1830s, lies beneath the lovely Soutpansberg range. The hills, mantled by dense natural forests and plantations of exotic trees, are unusually well watered: some areas receive an annual rainfall of 2 000 mm.

A developing rural settlement (*left*) in the heavily populated Lebowa region of the northern Transvaal. Forestry and citrus are among the local industries; the half-million citrus trees of the giant Zebediela estates produce more than 500 million oranges a year.

The Kruger National Park is South Africa's premier game reserve. Nearly 20 000 km² in extent, it occupies much of the Eastern Transvaal's Lowveld region, and is haven for a greater variety of wildlife than any other sanctuary in Africa. Mammal species alone number 137; bird species nearly 500.

47

ORANGE FREE STATE

ORANGE FREE STATE

The Golden Gate Highlands National Park, in the valley of the Little Caledon river beneath the towering mountains of Lesotho, is a scenically spectacular area of ramparts and ridges, peaks, cliffs and strangely sculpted rock formations. The shapes, many of them, are eye-catching; so too are the colours, especially when seen in the slanting light of dawn or at sunset: iron oxides have combined with the sandstone to create a vivid canvas of golden browns and muted reds, oranges and yellows.

This is the far eastern segment of the Orange Free State, a landlocked, 120 000-km^2 slice of the high central plateau sandwiched between the Orange and Vaal rivers. Its principal centre – and South Africa's judicial capital – is Bloemfontein, a handsome if rather sombre city that began life in the mid-19th century as a tiny British military outpost and residency, and grew up, quietly and gracefully, around its flat-topped naval Hill. Around the turn of the century a visiting traveller described the town as 'one of the neatest and, in a modest way, best appointed capitals in the world. Gardens are planted with trees that are now so tall as to make the whole place swim in green'.

The landscapes around the Golden Gate are by no means typical of the province. Most of the Orange Free State is plains country, flat, windswept, bitterly cold in winter, bare of trees and natural features, though here and there the visual monotony is relieved by dykes and sills – dolerate outcrops known as *kopjes*. Rainfall is generally low, especially

so in the bleaker western reaches; the streams and the smaller rivers flow sporadically, in keeping with the seasons; surface water is scarce. For all its apparent harshness, though, the land is bountiful – immensely so. The Orange Free State produces about a third of South Africa's maize and wheat harvests; underground moisture and the good earth sustain great numbers of sheep and cattle. The region's wealth runs even deeper: in addition to its agricultural abundance the Orange Free State has massive mineral resources.

The gold mines around the young city of Welkom, to the north, account for about a third of the national output, and the earth also yields diamonds and platinum – and massive deposits of coal, whose exploitation gave birth (in 1954) to South Africa's first giant synthetic fuel plant, at Sasolburg, close to the Vaal river.

The massive, weathered formations of the Golden Gate Highlands National Park in the eastern Orange Free State (*previous page*) are an eye-catching array of autumn colours.

Bloemfontein's old market building (*above*) and strikingly innovative civic centre (*right*). Among the more notable of the city's finer edifices are the Fourth Raadsaal, completed in 1893 to serve as the last seat of the Boer republican government, and the Old Residency, stately home to three presidents of the Orange Free State.

The maize lands around Welkom (*above*), after harvesting. The Orange Free State, despite its generally low rainfall, produces about one third of South Africa's output of maize and wheat, and its grazing supports huge numbers of cattle and sheep.

Welkom (*right*), the Orange Free State's second largest urban concentration, was laid out in 1947 as a model township to serve the gold mines of the northern region. Features of the city are its pleasant parks, its pans (where thousands of water birds congregate), and its easily negotiable thoroughfares: vehicular flow is regulated by an impressive 23 traffic circles.

The still waters of the Hendrik Verwoerd dam on the Orange river (*far left*), the Orange Free State's southern boundary, are a magnet for dinghy and power-boat enthusiasts. This is South Africa's biggest reservoir, having a storage capacity of about 6 billion m^3 and covering an area of 374 km^2. The reserve on its northern shore is sanctuary for the country's largest herd of springbok, and for a breeding herd of the once rare mountain zebra.

The small town of Winburg (*left*), the original capital of the Orange Free State. It was founded in 1841 (when the territory was known as Trans-Orangia) and named, not in commemoration of a military exploit but of triumph in an argument about where precisely the village should be sited. On the farm Rietfontein, is an impressive Voortrekker monument and museum complex.

Harrismith (*left and above*), the eastern Orange Free State's largest town and a major centre on the highway between Johannesburg and the Natal coastal resorts, is set in a scenically stunning upland region. Close by is the Platberg, a distinctive height much favoured by hikers and picnickers, and the Harrismith Botanic Garden, which contains more than a thousand floral species occuring in the Drakensberg range to the south.

NATAL

A seagull's-eye view of a segment of Durban's famed Golden Mile (*previous page*), a 6-km stretch of graceful seafront that contains virtually everything the privileged pleasure-seeker could wish for: sea, surf and golden sand; lawns, fountains, pavilions, piers, pools and parks; round-the-clock eateries, discos and entertainment centres; glittering emporiums and some of Africa's largest and most elegant hotels.

The Oriental Plaza (*right*), one of Durban's major Indian market complexes, lends a touch of the traditional East to this most modern of cities. Here, stalls are crammed with brass, silver and gold, crafts and curios, sumptuous silks and satins – all bought and bartered for in an atmosphere aromatic with spices and sandalwood, incense and rose.

Part of Durban's colourful Golden Mile (*opposite*). One of the area's prime attractions is Seaworld, a splendid aquarium and dolphinarium housing a huge number and variety of tropical fish, turtles and stingrays, dolphins, seals, penguins, sharks, and a colourful array of corals and anemones. Behind the popular displays, though, is serious scientific purpose: a great deal of successful research is undertaken here.

NATAL

It has been called the Garden Province, and with justice: Natal is the smallest and arguably the most beautiful of South Africa's four provincial divisions, a pleasant land of rich soils and green hills, and of a tropically lush, infinitely varied plant life that is at its most colourful along the 600-kilometre coastline that runs from Transkei in the south to Kosi Bay and the Mozambique border in the north. The region's seaboard, indeed, is one of the southern hemisphere's most enticing playgrounds, numbering among its drawcards a balmy climate, beaches that are wide, golden and often palm-fringed, the glittering attractions of Durban, and scores of little resort towns, villages and hamlets that hug the shores of the bays, lagoons and river estuaries. Many of South Africa's finest game reserves lie along the northern shores and their immediate hinterland.

Durban is Natal's largest city and leading holiday centre, though not its capital. That honour belongs to Pietermaritzburg, a place of mellow red-brick buildings set in the higher, cooler country some 90 kilometres to the west. Farther inland the countryside rises to the foothills of the Drakensberg, a massive and, in geological terms, comparatively young chain of heights, formed 150 million years ago by a series of seismic convulsions and eroded over the millennia by wind, rain and river, elements that carved out deep gorges and sculpted an extraordinary fantasia of buttress and cliff, pinnacle and saw-edged ridge. The caves and overhangs of the Drakensberg and their foothills contain some of the country's most impressive 'galleries' of San (or Bushman) paintings, for it was here that these gentle people, finest of all prehistoric artists, sought refuge from their more numerous, and more aggressive, Bantu-speaking fellow men. It was their ideal home: the cavern-studded ravines offered fresh water, access to the game-rich grasslands to the east, and protection against both human depredation and the elements. The Bushmen have long since disappeared from the region, but their artistic legacy remains everywhere to delight the modern eye.

Durban's central business district, with the Edwardian city hall (*above*), which was modelled on that of Belfast, Northern Ireland, and completed in 1910. A multi-million rand upgrading programme is preparing the city – South Africa's third largest and one of the fastest growing in the world – for the 21st century.

Durban's Victoria Embankment (*above and following pages*) and its small-craft harbour. Among the features of the area are the Natal Maritime Museum, the African Arts Centre, the impressively intricate Vasco Da Gama Clock, and the pleasure cruisers that take one out into the bay and from which one can enjoy wave-bobbing views of the city.

Greater Durban is home to a great many Indian people, some of them direct descen-
dants of the first indentured labourers brought in, during the 1860s, to work the vast sugar
plantations of the region. The community is a remarkably integrated one, generally prosperous,
organized according to faith (Hindu and Muslim) and underpinned by the *kutum* – the disciplined
extended family structure. Pictured (*above*) is a mosque in the Cato Manor area.

ariannhill (*left*), in the Pinetown area near Durban, is an impressive complex of monastery, convent, college, orphanage and hospital, founded in 1882 and run, during its first quarter-century, by Trappist monks. It was taken over by the Mariannhill Missionaries in 1909.

Pietermaritzburg *(right)*, the capital of Natal, is a charming city of red-brick Victorian buildings, cast-iron storefronts, alleyways and antique shops, gardens bright with roses and azaleas – and a number of impressive modern edifices. The new co-exists comfortably with the old.

Hilton College (*above*), on the beautiful woodland escarpment above the city of Pietermaritzburg, is one of the country's best-known private educational establishments, modelled on the older and more fashionable 'public' schools of England. It was founded in the early 1870s by the Reverend W.O. Newnham.

The field of Blood River (*above*), with its commemorative *laager* of replica ox-wagons. Here, on 16 December 1838, the eastern Voortrekkers, led by Andries Pretorius, finally and decisively defeated Dingane's Zulu army in a battle where numbers and courage proved less than a match for disciplined firepower. Some 3 000 warriors died on the battlefield; just three of Pretorius's men were wounded.

The Valley of a Thousand Hills (*right*) is a massive, majestically rugged area that follows the course of the Mgeni River for 65 km, from the flat-topped heights of Natal Table Mountain near Pietermaritzburg eastward to the Indian Ocean. In some parts it is heavily populated, in others it remains an unspoilt Eden of green-mantled hill, ravine and wide vista. Among the area's tourist venues is Phezulu, a village complex featuring traditional life styles.

The graceful Howick Falls (*above*), to the north-west of Pietermaritzburg and near the pleasant town of Howick, plunge 95 m into a gorge of the Umgeni river. The most convenient natural ford is just above the falls and, in the early days, many a traveller was swept to his death by the sometimes treacherous waters. A bridge now spans the river at this point.

North of Pietermaritzburg is the 1 822-ha Midmar dam (*right*), a popular recreation venue for boating, fishing and for bathing in the bilharzia-free waters. The Midmar historical village features, among other things, a traditional Zulu homestead and a wood-and-iron Hindu temple.

The Drakensberg range of mountains (*opposite and above*) fall almost sheer for a full 2 000 m to the foothills below. Along the entire 250 km length of the main rampart there is just one roadway – over the 3 200-m Sani Pass into the kingdom of Lesotho.

The distinctively shaped Bell (*top*), part of the Cathedral Peak complex of pinnacles. Cathedral Peak itself rises 3 004 m above sea level, but is one of the region's more accessible heights.

Lake Sibaya (*above*), South Africa's largest freshwater lake – it covers 77 km^2 of Natal's northern coastal plain – is separated from the Indian Ocean by a high and narrow belt of forested dunes. The deep (30 m) waters of the lake are famed for their crystal clarity. Wildlife includes crocodile and hippo, reedbuck, jackal and nearly 300 species of bird.

Sodwana Bay National Park (*top*), comprising about 400 ha of beach, dune, marsh and lake on the Tongaland (northern Natal) coast, is one of the region's most visited reserves.

Tsonga fishing traps, linked together by 'stakes' of reeds and branches, in the waters of Kosi Bay (*above*), one of a graceful sequence of Zululand lakes and lagoons.

One of the largest and most remarkable of Africa's marine wildernesses is St Lucia (*left*), a splendid complex of lake, lily-covered pan, game reserve, dune-forest, river estuary and seashore. The shallow lake, in reality a series of lagoons, sustains hippo and crocodile and a wonderfully rich bird life that includes white pelicans, saddlebill storks, Caspian terns, flamingos, twelve species of heron and a breeding community of fish eagles. There are plans to expand the complex to create a 275 000-ha Greater St Lucia Conservation Area.

Dune-mining at St Lucia (*above*). The practice, and plans to strip-mine titanium in the Eastern Shores nature reserve (part of the St Lucia complex), have provoked a massive public outcry. The scheme has been shelved for the time being.

Richards Bay (*above*), on the northern Natal coast, is a comparatively new deep-water port. It came on stream only in 1976, but now ranks as South Africa's busiest harbour in terms of cargo volume handled. Most of the throughput comprises bulk commodities (phosphates, pig-iron and ferro-alloys feature prominently); the coal terminal is the world's largest.

The Mdloti river mouth divides the two beachfront resorts of Umdloti and Tongaat Beach.

The seaboard north of Durban – the 100-km stretch to the Tugela river-mouth – is known as the Dolphin Coast, an area noted for its broad beaches, for a tropical shoreline graced by a profusion of hibiscuses, casuarinas, bougainvillea, lala palms and a wealth of other colourful trees and shrubs, and for its quiet little resort villages. Pictured (*above*) is Ballito, a place of modern timeshare complexes and fashionable holiday homes.

Just to the north of Durban is Umhlanga Rocks, one of the country's most popular holiday areas. It boasts four luxurious hotels (including the famed Oyster Box (*top*)), modern apartment blocks, graceful villas and a fine beach. The upmarket La Lucia residential suburb falls within the Umhlanga municipal boundaries.

Umdloti Beach (*above*) is one of the more highly developed of the north-coast resorts: it has two modern hotels, and is popular for its lagoon and lovely expanse of sand. The name is taken from a type of wild tobacco that grows along the Mdloti river. The waters off the entire eastern seaboard are home to an intimidating number and variety of sharks, but at many places – among them Umdloti – bathers, surfers and ski-boaters are protected by nets.

Natal's south coast (*right*) is a tropical paradise; the balmy climate, the warm and intensely blue waters of the ocean, the lushly evergreen hinterland and the sunlit resort villages are a magnet for holidaymakers, affluent retirees and for city-dwellers rich and leisured enough to afford a second home. The 170-km shoreline is divided into two segments (a rather arbitrary distinction, but a useful one for publicity purposes) – the Sunshine Coast, which runs from Amanzimtoti to Mtwalume, and the Hibiscus Coast, which ends at Port Edward, on the Transkei border.

Largest of southern Natal's rivers is the uMzimkhulu, which rises in the high Drakensberg to the north-west and flows for 320 km before discharging into the ocean at Port Shepstone (*opposite*), a substantial south-coast town centred on the sugar, timber, tropical fruit and marble industries and on the local limeworks. The river is navigable by small craft for about 10 km upstream from its wide estuary. The area's attractions include splendid beaches, tidal pools and tree-shaded parks; the golf course ranks among South Africa's finest.

Scottburgh's tidal pool (*right*). Among the attractions in and around the town, one of the more prominent along the Sunshine Coast, is an 18-hole golf course, bowling greens, and an unusually large salt-water pool. Nearby is a splendid miniature railway, and Crocworld which, apart from its crocodiles, also encompasses a wildlife museum and a living exhibition of Zulu culture.

Banana plantations in the southern Natal hinterland (*below*). The plant was imported into Natal soon after the first white settlers began to spread out through the interior during the mid 19th century. The bananas are harvested while still green and then ripened under controlled conditions.

The Oribi Gorge (*far right*), a massive canyon carved from the sandstone layers of the southern Natal coastal region by the Umzimkulwana river. The gorge, 24 km long, five kilometres at its widest and up to 366 m deep, is the centrepiece of a 2 000-ha nature reserve that serves as sanctuary for some 40 species of mammal, though the graceful and now fairly rare antelope from which the name was taken is no longer present.

Perhaps the Transkei Wild Coast's best-known physical feature is the Hole in the Wall (*left*), a massive detached cliff through whose arched opening the surf thunders. Its local name, *esiKhaleni*, means 'place of sound'. Two kilometres away is the Hole in the Wall hotel and holiday village; a pleasant walk along the coast will bring you to Coffee Bay.

Transkei's beautiful, though sometimes treacherous, Indian Ocean shoreline is known as the Wild Coast, a 254-km long stretch of imposing cliffs, reefs, sandy coves, lagoons and estuaries that extends from the Mtamvuna river in the east to the Great Kei river bordering the eastern Cape Province. Pictured (*above*) are the precipitous faces of Cathedral Rock.

The Transkei seaboard is a densely populated area, but several segments have been proclaimed as conservation areas and stocked with game. Among them are the Mkambati and Dwesa reserves, attractive expanses of evergreen forest, grassland, rocky shore and long stretches of sandy beach.

The neat little lighthouse complex at Port St Johns, on Transkei's Wild Coast (*above*). The settlement takes its name from one of the most tragic shipwrecks of the pre-colonial era, that of the Portuguese vessel *St John*, which came to grief in 1552. The 440 survivors, some of them of noble rank, set out on foot for the island of Mocambique, 1 600 km to the north-east; just 25 finally staggered to safety.

Port St Johns (*right*) lies at the Umzimvubu river estuary in a magnificent setting of towering headland, forest and golden-fringed ocean, and is one of the Wild Coast's principal holiday spots. Its Second Beach (there are three) is the site of a 'cottage colony'; a fair sprinkling of artists and writers have made their permanent home in the area.

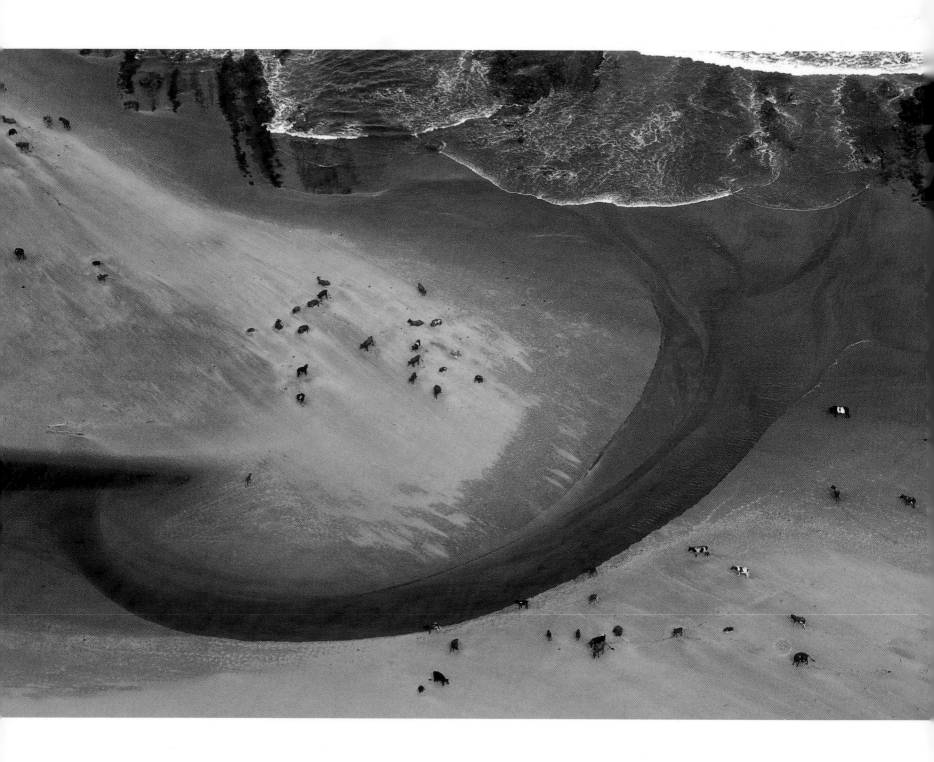

The Transkei region has a population of some three million and covers an area of 42 000 km², most of it rolling, grass-covered upland terrain dotted with rondavel-type Xhosa homesteads (many, curiously, built with their doors facing east). Pictured (*above*) is the fairly heavily settled countryside inland from Coffee Bay.

Xhosa cattle cluster around a small river estuary on the Transkei's golden shores (*left*). Pastoral farming is the region's principal economic activity.

CAPE PROVINCE

CAPE PROVINCE

Early Portuguese seafarers called it *Cabo Tormentoso* – the Cape of Storms – but it later became known as the Cape of Good Hope, a kindlier and more optimistic name for the southernmost African coasts and, in particular, for the massive promontory at the tip of a peninsula that probes, fingerlike, into the wild blue waters of the Atlantic. At the other end of the peninsula is the immense, flat-topped bulk of Table Mountain, and it was here, on the shores of the bay below the heights, that the first European colonists made their landfall. Over the centuries their settlement, Cape Town, developed into a graceful metropolis that eventually became (in 1910) the seat of the national legislature – and capital of South Africa's largest provincial division.

The Cape covers rather more than half the country's land area – 641 000 square kilometres in all, which is just a little smaller than the state of Texas, and much of it is taken up by the Great Karoo, an arid-looking, mostly featureless land of far horizons, of clear skies and bone-dry air, of blistering daytime heat and, in winter, bitter nights. Here, one feels, only the hardiest life forms are able to survive. But appearances are deceptive: there is good underground water and this, together with the sweet grasses of the eastern plains, sustain half a dozen small towns, a scatter of lonely fishing hamlets and a high proportion of the country's 27 million herd of sheep.

Beyond lies the diamond city of Kimberley and, farther west, the immense wastelands of Gordonia, the Kalahari, and the Cape's Atlantic seaboard. These western regions receive very little rain and the countryside is, for the most part and for most of the year, a bleak desolation of sand and scrub. But the Cape has other and more benevolent faces. The best soils, and the largest concentrations of people, are to be found in the coastal belt that extends from the Peninsula and its lovely, vine-covered hinterland eastwards through Ciskei to the river-port of East London in what is known as the Border area. Running parallel to the coast is a series of mountain ranges which at no point quite touch the shore: uplands and sea are separated by a narrow plain renowned for its scenic splendour and its enormously rich plant life. One 230-kilometre stretch, the celebrated Garden Route that runs from Mossel Bay to Storms River, is especially notable: on one side is the Indian Ocean, the coastline a stunning progression of cliff and rocky cove, lagoon, broad embayment and golden sand; on the other the thickly forested slopes of the Outeniqua and Tsitsikamma mountains and, between the two, is the fertile and stunningly beautiful garden terrace. The towns and villages of these maritime regions are generally a lot older than those of the country's northern parts; most have aged gracefully, each has its own character and distinction. Cape Town is famed for its magnificent mountain setting; Stellenbosch is the largest and, with its oak-lined avenues and stately edifices, arguably the most attractive of the wineland centres. George, at the western end of the Garden Route, has its green valleys and hills; Knysna and Wilderness their lakes; Port Elizabeth, capital of the eastern Cape, its industrial muscle, its wide beaches and its splendid harbour.

The Bloukrans River Bridge (*previous page*) is one of three magnificent river crossings in the Plettenberg Bay area of the Cape's famed Garden Route. Each offers fine vistas; the Bloukrans is 425-m long and traverses the gorge at a dizzying 270 m above the riverbed.

The Cape coastal city of East London (*right*), situated at the mouth of the Buffalo river and South Africa's only major river port. The city's museum has two specially notable exhibits: the world's only surviving dodo's egg, and the first coelacanth to be caught in recent times.

The capital of the eastern Cape region is Port Elizabeth (*left*), a handsome city that has its origins in the landing of 4 000 British settlers on the shores of Algoa Bay in 1820. The most prominent of the area's many industries is motor manufacturing, though tourism is becoming increasingly important to the local economy. Port Elizabeth's nicknames, 'Friendly City', 'Windy City' and 'Detroit of South Africa' reflect its many-sided personality.

Much of Port Elizabeth's more pleasing architecture reflects the city's British origins. Among the survivors from the city's adolescence are elegant Regency-type homes, Victorian villas with filigree balustrades and verandahs, and rows of charming terraced houses (*above*).

The lighthouse on Bird Island (*top*), off the shores of Algoa Bay. The island is home to the world's largest community of gannets. The birds crowd together in dense breeding colonies, each nest of sticks, seaweed and guano built just out of pecking range of its neighbour.

Dolphins sporting in the warm waters of Algoa Bay (*top*). A number of these appealing marine mammals are kept in Port Elizabeth's renowned Oceanarium, where they perform entertainingly in the enormous (nearly five million litre) pool.

The Swartkops river (*above*), which reaches the sea some 10 km west of Port Elizabeth, is a popular recreation venue; the waters are navigable for 18 km upstream. There are fine beaches around the estuary, and a number of pleasant riverside resorts.

Cape Recife (*above*), a gentle promontory that probes into the Indian Ocean just to the south of Port Elizabeth. The dune-fringed shoreline is fragile, vulnerable to human encroachment (the city's popular Summerstrand beach is next door), and the area has been proclaimed as a nature reserve. Sea and shore are home to innumerable birds.

The Storms river rises in the Tsitsikamma region of the southern marginal rampart and flows through enchanting forest country to reach the ocean at the eastern end of the Garden Route (*right*). The area's narrow coastal plateau, the shoreline, and the sea for a distance of five kilometres have been proclaimed as the Tsitsikamma National Park, one of the southern hemisphere's most fascinating marine reserves.

Fertile farmlands grace the countryside inland from Tsitsikamma (*far right*). The dense woodlands in the distance, a remnant of the once-vast natural forests of the southern Cape, are home to stinkwood and white alder, assegai, candlewood, ironwood, giant Outeniqua yellowwoods (which can grow over 50 m in height) and many other magnificent tree species.

Plettenberg Bay's Beacon Island (*left*), once the site of a whaling station, now supports a sophisticated hotel and timeshare complex. The town – one of South Africa's most fashionable resort centres – has a scenically spectacular setting, three superb beaches, and its residents enjoy a full 320 days of virtually uninterrupted sunshine each year.

The aptly named Nature's Valley (*above*), a holiday village and reserve at the foot of the Groot River Pass on the southern Cape coast. The valley, in a lovely setting of sea, lagoon, river and dense woodland, is surrounded on three sides by the Tsitsikamma state forest reserve.

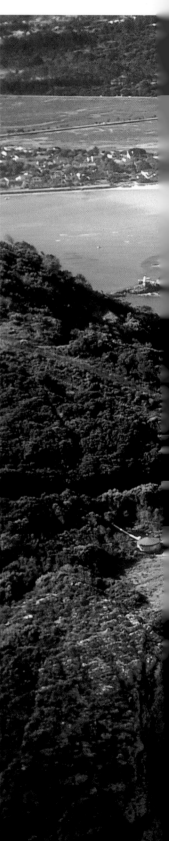

Workers in transit across the Knysna lagoon (*right*). Visitors are offered more leisurely style; the choices range from sailing dinghies through to luxurious cabin cruisers.

Below Knysna's eastern Head is Leisure Island (*above*), a charming residential area connected to the mainland by a causeway. For holidaymakers, there are two hotels, golden sands, and the clear, warm waters of a lagoon.

The Knysna and neighbouring Wilderness areas are South Africa's 'Lake District', a scenically spectacular region of sea, lagoon, mountain and forest. At the ocean entrance to Knysna's lagoon are The Heads (*right*), two imposing sandstone cliffs. The western Head accommodates the Featherbed Bay private nature reserve.

The causeway linking the green-garlanded shores of Knysna lagoon (*far left*). This view is from the Belvidere area, the spacious and splendidly wooded 19th-century estate of the Duthie family. Its small Norman-style chapel was described by Bishop Gray, who consecrated it in 1855, as 'the most perfect yet in the diocese'.

Pine plantations mantle the hills near Knysna (*left*). The region is better known for its indigenous forests, the country's largest expanse of natural woodland. They are home to a wide variety of magnificent tree species and, in the Knysna area, to the pitifully few survivors of the once-prolific herds of Cape elephant.

Graaff-Reinet (*far left*), founded in 1786 in a sweeping loop of the Sundays River beneath the grandeur of Spandau Kop, is known as 'the gem of the Karoo': more than 200 of its beautifully designed and crafted old buildings have been restored and proclaimed as national monuments, including the elegant Drostdy, or magistrate's residence and court. The latter, together with a cluster of adjoining cottages, now serves as a hotel complex.

The Swartberg range (*left*), to the north of the Little Karoo flatlands, is a spectacular chain of mountain heights sliced through by precipitous passes and deep kloofs. The summit of Swartberg Pass, which links Oudtshoorn with Prince Albert on the fringe of the Great Karoo, is snow-mantled in winter, glorious with wild flowers in summer.

The Karoo town of Colesberg (*far right*), on the national route almost precisely half way between Johannesburg and Cape Town, was founded in 1829 and, shortly thereafter, played a significant part in the Great Trek (it was home to several of the Trek's more prominent personalities). The town is now the centre of a thriving local sheep-farming industry; the region's mutton is said to be the country's tastiest.

'Capital' of the Great Karoo is Beaufort West (*right*), an attractive town of refreshingly green suburban gardens and pear tree-lined streets. The Karoo receives very little rain, but there is good underground water in the eastern parts of the region, the grasses are sweet, and these two elements combine to sustain enormous flocks of sheep.

Upington (*left*), principal town of the huge scrubland and semi-desert district of Gordonia, is set on the north bank of the Orange river, serving as a major railhead (the line reaches town via a 1 067 m bridge) and air communications centre (the airport's main runway, at 5,5 km, is the southern hemisphere's longest). Among local products are karakul sheep, wool, dried fruit, dates, and, curiously enough, wine.

The Big Hole (*above*), diamond-rich Kimberley's most striking feature. This was the original mine, the first of four giant kimberlite 'pipes' found in this part of the northern Cape and before it was closed, in 1914, it had reached a depth of 1 098 m (which ranked it, until recently, as the world's largest man-made crater). During its 43-year lifespan it yielded three tons of precious stones; today, silent and half-filled with water, it forms part of Kimberley's outstandingly evocative mine museum. Other mines still operate in the area.

The bleak sandveld plains of the Namaqualand near Springbok (*far left*). During most of the year this dry and often forbidding western Cape coastal region seems incapable of sustaining any but the hardiest, least attractive forms of life, but for a few weeks in springtime the country-side is transformed by glorious carpets of wild flowers.

Some 120 km to the west of Upington the Orange river flows through the narrow, 18-km long Augrabies canyon in a spectacular sequence of rapids and cascades, then breaches the rim of the main gorge to fall in a thunderous roar of cataracts into a rock-enclosed pool some 200 m below. The Augrabies Falls (*left*), which rank among the world's six largest waterfalls, are within an 80 000-ha national park.

Lamberts Bay (*left*) has one of the west coast's larger harbours, and is a major centre of the once-thriving fishing industry. Over-exploitation during the past decade has depleted the marine resources, however, and the town is becoming increasingly dependent on tourism. The area attracts bird-watchers (the bay and its 'island' are haven to huge colonies of sea birds), yachtsmen and sport-fishermen; amenities include an excellent hotel, seafood eateries, and a rather windswept seafront.

Bird's-eye-view of the lighthouse complex (*above right*) in the Cape Columbine Nature Reserve, three kilometres along the coast from Paternoster. This generates an impressive nine-million candlepower, and on clear nights the light – the first seen by voyagers taking the western sea route from Europe – can be discerned 40 km out to sea.

The charming little fishing hamlet of Paternoster takes its name from the heartfelt prayer of thanksgiving offered up by a party of early ship-wreck survivors. The area tends to draw the quieter kind of holiday-maker. The rocks (*right*) are a happy hunting ground for crayfishermen.

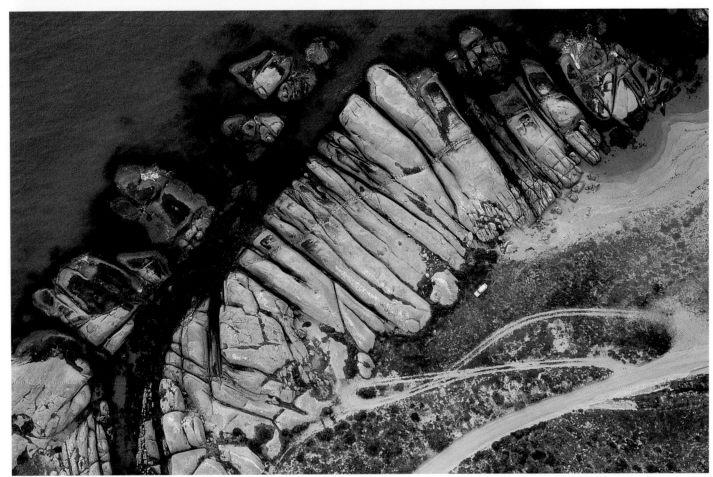

Inland from the Cape west coast the terrain rises to the heights of the Cedarberg (*above*), a ruggedly beautiful mountain range that is named after the rare and at one time almost extinct Clanwilliam cedar tree. The region is distinguished by its stark and strangely eroded rock formations, its caverns and overhangs, its perennial streams, waterfalls and crystal pools, and its floral splendour and magnificent vistas. This is a proclaimed wilderness area, accessible on a controlled basis to hikers and campers.

The Ceres basin (*right*), among the mountains to the south of the Cedarberg, is appropriately named after the Roman goddess of agriculture: it is one of the country's most bountiful, and most beautiful, fruit-growing areas, yielding splendid harvests of apples, pears, peaches and nectarines, and vast quantities of potatoes as well. The headwater streams of the Breede River gather here to join and flow south-eastwards through the Cape's famed winelands.

Saldanha Bay (*left*), with its superb natural harbour, is the head-quarters of the west coast fishing industry, and a deep-water terminal for the export of iron ore, brought in over a specially constructed, 860-km electrified railway from Sishen in the northern Cape. The port, which can accommodate the largest of bulk carriers, is geared to handle 33 million tons of ore a year.

An ostrich in full flight across the sands of the Postberg Nature Reserve (*above right*), part of the much larger West Coast National Park. The park's principal feature is the relatively shallow, 16-km long Langebaan lagoon, which, together with the mudbanks and sandbanks of the area and Saldanha Bay's rocky shores and islands, attract tens of thousands of waders and other bird species.

The pretty little west-coast hinterland village of Philadelphia (*right*), meaning 'brotherly love' (the reference taken from the Book of Revelations). It was once known as Koeberg, now the name of the nearby site of South Africa's only nuclear power complex.

Cape Town's 'northern suburbs' in fact lie to the east. Bellville (*opposite*) is a large industrial and residential centre, and a city in its own right, set below the slopes of the Tygerberg hills. The neighbouring suburb of Parow is the site of the renowned Tygerberg Hospital.

The seaside village of Melkbosstrand (*above*), to the north of Cape Town, is named after the local milkwood tree, a handsome and carefully protected species. The area is well patronized by sea-anglers and crayfish divers, and also serves as the venue for energetic *boeresport* gatherings – traditional Afrikaans-speaking get-togethers – each New Year.

Robben Island (*left*), nine kilometres off the shore of Table Bay, achieved notoriety during the apartheid years as a State prison for political prisoners, though it had served, sporadically, as a convict settlement and repository for 'undesirables' since the 16th century. There are proposals to develop the area as a nature reserve and memorial.

The detached Woodbridge Island area (*below*) of the Cape Town suburb of Milnerton, named in honour of former British High Commissioner and arch-Imperialist Lord Milner. The nearby bridge across the seasonally flowing Salt river takes northward-bound motorists past lagoon, beach, the pleasant Milnerton racecourse and Rietvlei, sanctuary for a fascinating array of water birds.

C ape Town panorama
(*left*). In the background is the massively distinctive bulk of Table Mountain, in the foreground the pentagonal Castle of Good Hope, the oldest occupied building in South Africa. It was built during the decade between 1666 and 1676, and served thereafter as the Cape Governor's official residence and military headquarters. It now functions, in part, as a museum.

Yachts at their moorings in Cape Town's harbour (*opposite top*). The older part of the harbour – the Victoria and Alfred basins – is being transformed through a multi-billion rand redevelopment scheme, and the area promises to rival Table Mountain as the city's premier tourist attraction.

The massive Victoria and Alfred Waterfront project (*opposite*) takes its inspiration from other, highly successful redevelopment schemes around the world, but is tailored to suit Cape Town's particular needs and distinctive character. Some of the old harbour buildings are being converted, and new ones built, to serve as hotels, restaurants, pubs, fish-, produce- and craft-markets, speciality shops, cinemas, entertainment centres and museums. Marinas, open quaysides, promenades, jetties, public squares, walkways, waterways, an oceanarium, offices and apartments, all feature in the plans.

Cape Town's principal thoroughfare is the Heerengracht (*left*), which begins at the harbour and extends elegantly across the Foreshore (a large tract of land reclaimed from the sea) towards Table Mountain, changing its name to Adderley Street half way along. The tall building on the left is part of the Sanlam Golden Acre which, together with adjacent above- and below-ground concourses, comprises one of Africa's largest shopping complexes. The area, once close to the seashore, is believed to be the site of Jan van Riebeeck's first earth-and-timber fort, built in 1652.

Part of the campus of the University of Cape Town (*opposite*), set on the slopes of Table Mountain beneath Devil's Peak. The university's student enrolment stands at about 14 000; its medical faculty, whose teaching facility is neighbouring Groote Schuur Hospital, is renowned.

One of Cape Town's more prominent landmarks is Mostert's Mill (*left*), on the De Waal Drive motorway that runs through the University of Cape Town campus. The mill, built in 1796, was restored during the 1930s.

Claremont, among Cape Town's most prestigious suburbs, is fast becoming a mecca for shoppers. Pictured (*below left*) is the Cavendish Square complex of speciality outlets, restaurants, art and exhibition centres.

*S*ea Point (above), close to the city, is a crowded, cosmopolitan, highrise suburb and the nearest thing Cape Town has to a holiday playground. Luxurious apartment blocks line Beach Road, its elegant, palm-graced seafront highway; hotels, restaurants, discos and delis are everywhere. Beach Road runs into Victoria Drive, one of the Cape's most splendid scenic routes: it follows the Peninsula's western shoreline to Hout Bay, 15 km to the south.

Mouille Point (*right*) close to Cape Town, is distinguished by its lighthouse, the oldest in the country (it dates from 1824). Today the 850 000-candlepower lamp can be seen 23 km out to sea, and the foghorn keeps the area's flat-dwellers awake at night.

Hout Bay's harbour and town nestle in a wide, green valley beneath the wooded mountain slopes (*opposite top*). Fisheries (snoek, rock lobster) and tourism are the two main local industries. Attractions include the inviting Mariner's Wharf development, modelled on its San Francisco namesake, and the World of Birds, the country's largest complex of aviaries, where some 450 different species can be found. The distinctively shaped peak in the foreground is known as the Sentinel.

The scenically stunning 10-km Chapman's Peak Drive (*opposite*) skirts the mountain between Hout Bay and low-lying Noordhoek on the Peninsula's western seaboard. At the road's highest point the cliffs fall down, almost sheer, to the Atlantic Ocean 600 m below; the views are splendid.

Cape Point (*left*), on the southern tip of the Peninsula, is a place of towering sandstone buttress and breathtaking vista – and of legend. It is around this massive headland that the *Flying Dutchman*, the ghostly, storm-swept ship with its deserted decks, is destined to sail until the end of time. The Point lies within the Cape of Good Hope Nature Reserve, established principally to conserve the local *fynbos*, a unique and botanically remarkable heath-type vegetation.

'White as the sands of Muizenberg,' wrote Rudyard Kipling, 'spun before the gale'. And indeed the beaches close to this False Bay resort are both windswept and beautiful. The town itself (*left*), the mecca of leisure-bent Victorians and still popular among casual holiday-makers, remains rather old-fashioned in character, full of turn-of-the-century villas, seaside boarding houses and converted fishermen's cottages.

Khayelitsha (*above*) means 'new home', and was established in the 1980s to house the people of Crossroads and other poverty-stricken 'squatter' settlements on the desolate Cape Flats to the east of Cape Town. In the early 1990s the township accommodated something over a quarter of a million residents – still a relatively small proportion of those in need of decent shelter.

On the seaward side of Somerset West lies Strand (*left*) a resort town popular for its gently shelving sands and its splendid holiday amenities. The area also has a solid industrial base which includes, among several other enterprises, food processing plants, and a chemicals and dynamite factory.

To the east of Strand is the charming little coastal village of Gordon's Bay (*opposite*), much favoured by Capetonian weekenders and, increasingly, by retired people seeking a quiet life in idyllic surrounds.

On the scenically lovely Houw Hoek Pass road that leads eastwards from the mountains is the Houw Hoek Inn (*top*), the oldest licenced hotel in South Africa (the main house dates from about 1870).

Just beyond the Hottentots Holland range, in the Overberg region, the farmlands (**above**) yield the country's largest crops of apples and pears, peaches and much else besides. Headquarters of the local fruit industry are the two small centres of Elgin and Grabouw.

In the hills above Gordon's Bay is the 380-ha Steenbras dam (*right*), an important source of water for Cape Town and other centres, and a splendid resort and recreational area.

The small town of Franschhoek – 'French glen' – huddles among the vineyards of the lovely Drakenstein valley (*below*), and was founded in 1688, on land granted to a party of French Huguenots from strife-torn Europe.

The Taalmonument, (the Afrikaans language monument), at Paarl (*left*). This is the largest of the south-western Cape's inland centres and a town noted for its unusually long oak- and jacaranda-shaded main street, which runs a distance of 10 km from end to end; for its pleasant suburban gardens, and for its associations with the wine industry.

Stellenbosch (*far left*), beneath the wooded heights of the Papegaaiberg, is the country's second oldest and one of its most handsome towns. It was founded in 1679 and grew gracefully, in keeping with its setting; the early settlers planted a profusion of oak trees, laid out open spaces, and constructed thatch-roofed, lime-washed homes. Later, some splendid public buildings were built, among them those of the University of Stellenbosch. Much of this charming past has been preserved, best seen perhaps along Dorp Street and around Die Braak, the old village green. In the general area are some of the most attractive and best known Cape's vineyards, estates and historic homesteads.

Prosperous vineyards (*above*) mantle the lovely countryside around the historic town of Stellenbosch. The Stellenbosch wine route, modelled on the famed *Routes de Vin* of France and Germany's *Weinstrassen*, was the first to be established (in the early 1970s) and now takes in 17 private cellars and five co-operative wineries.

Boschendal (*right*), near Franschhoek, is one of the region's best-known and, in terms of tourism, best-loved wine estates. The Cape Flemish-style manor house, which dates from 1812, has been restored to its former elegance; the restaurant is famed for its traditional Cape cuisine.

At the entrance to the Hex river valley is Worcester (*opposite top*), a substantial town on the main north-south highway. Of special interest here is the open-air Klein-plasie museum, which re-creates the life and times of the early Dutch farmer, and the Karoo National Botanic Garden, internationally renowned for its array of succulents.

Tulbagh (*opposite*), in the Breede river valley, is one of the most pleasing of the south-western Cape's towns. It was founded as a frontier settlement in the early 1700s to grow, around the Old Church, into a place of charmingly picturesque buildings. Many were destroyed in the great earthquake of 1969, but have since been restored to their pristine 18th-century condition.

Montagu (*left*) and its surrounding farmlands, beneath the high mountains that fringe the Little Karoo, are known for their heavy, richly flavoured muskadel and fortified wines. The area is also famed for its mineral springs, 'discovered' by travellers some 200 years ago. The warm and soothing waters – they well up at a constant 43°C temperature – are now central to an attractive spa complex of hotels, time-share apartments and holiday cottages.

The mountain-fringed valley of the Hex river (*above*) sustains over 200 farms that, together, produce the great bulk of South Africa's late-maturing export grapes. The area is a magnet for hikers and mountaineers; some of the winter-time slopes provide a playground for skiers.

Close to the Riviersonderend range of hills in the Overberg is Greyton (*right*), a peaceful village that features an oak-lined main street, two old-fashioned and excellent hotels and, within the resident community, a liberal sprinkling of artists and writers. The Greyton nature reserve is worth visiting for its spectacular landscapes.

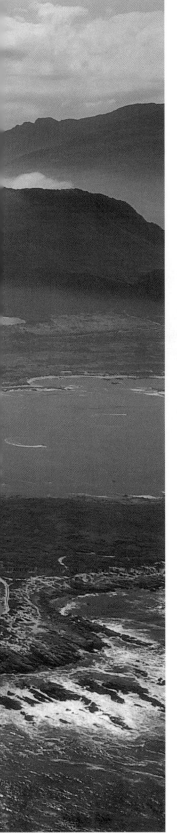

The Hottentots Holland mountains reach the sea at Cape Hangklip (*left*), the eastern extremity of False Bay. The area, once a refuge for fugitive slaves and cattle-rustlers, remains relatively unspoilt: human encroachment is confined to a scatter of cottages and a lighthouse.

Hermanus (*above*), is the Overberg's largest coastal centre and premier resort town, beautifully set between mountain and deep-blue sea. Among its attractions is the Old Harbour, once a hive of commercial fishing and whaling activity and now preserved as a museum. On view are vintage fishing boats and reconstructed buildings. The nearby Hamilton Russell vineyards are southern Africa's southernmost.

The charming thatched and whitewashed cottages of Waenhuiskrans (*right*), which translates as 'wagon house cliff – a reference to the enormous sea-cavern nearby. The village's alternative (unofficial, but popular) name is Arniston, commemorating one of the many shipwrecks along this often gale-blown coast. The local hotel is widely, and deservedly, renowned.

The fishing hamlet of Gansbaai – 'Goose Bay' – near Danger Point on the Cape south coast (*above*). It was off this headland that, in 1852, the British troopship *Birkenhead* was wrecked with the loss of 445 lives. Only three of the lifeboats proved serviceable; ranks of doomed soldiers stood to rigid attention as the ship foundered.

INDEX

Augrabies Falls 123

Ballito 82
Banana plantations, Natal 86
Beacon Island 106
Beaufort West 118
Bellville 130
Belvidere 110
Bird Island, Port Elizabeth 101
Bloemfontein 50, 51
Blood River 70
Bloukrans River Bridge 96-97
Bluff 8
BMW 20-21
Boksburg 6
Boschendal 151
Bruma 18

Cape Aghulas 160
Cape Columbine 125
Cape Hangklip 156
Cape Point 141
Cape Recife 103
Cape Town 133
Cathedral Rock 90
Cato Manor 66
Cattle, Transkei 94
Cavendish Square 137
Cedarberg 126
Ceres Basin 127
Chapman's Peak 140
Church Square, Pretoria 30
Coffee Bay, inland 95
Colesberg 119

Diagonal Street, 15
Dolobran House,
    Johannesburg 10-11
Dolphins 102
Drakensberg 74-75
Durban 4, 7
    beachfront 61
    CBD 62
    Golden Mile 58-59

East London 98-99
East Rand 22
Ebenezer Dam 43
Ellis Park, Johannesburg 13

Ferry, Knysna 108
Franschhoek 148

Gansbaai 159
George 115
Gold Reef City 19
Golden Gate 48-49
Gordon's Bay 144

Graaff Reinet 116
Grabouw 146
Grand Central Aerodrome 23
Greyton 155

Hartebeespoort Dam 32-33
Harrismith 56, 57
Heerengracht, Cape Town 135
Hendrik Verwoerd Dam 54
Hermanus 157
Hex River Valley 154
Hillbrow 12
Hilton College 69
Hole in the Wall, 88-89
Hout Bay 140
Houw Hoek 146
Howick Falls 72

Iscor 24-25

Johannesburg 2-3
Joubert Park 15

Khayelitsha 143
Kimberley 121
Knysna forests 111
Knysna Heads 109
Kosi Bay 77
Kroondal 36-37
Kruger National Park 46-47

Lake Sibaya 76
Lamberts Bay 124
Leisure Island 108
Louis Trichardt 44-45

Mac-Mac Falls 40
Magaliesberg 34
Marianhill 67
Melkbosstrand 131
Midmar Dam 73,
Mmabatho 38
Montagu 153
Mossel Bay 114
Mostert's Mill, Cape Town 137
Mouille Point 139
Muizenberg 142

Nature's Valley 107
Ndebele 40

Oribi Gorge 87
Oriental Plaza, Durban 60
Ostrich 129

Parktown 14
Parkview Golf Club 17
Paternoster 125
Phalaborwa 42
Philadelphia 129

Pietermaritzburg 68
Pietersburg 44-45
Port Elizabeth 100, 101
Port Shepstone 85
Port St Johns 92, 93
Power boat racing 18

Randburg 16
Richards Bay 80
Robben Island 132
Robbers Pass 41
Rustenburg 35

Saldanha Bay 128
Scottburgh 86
Sea Point 138
Sedgefield 112
Serpentine, Wilderness 113
Sodwana 77
South Coast, Natal 84
Springbok, near 122
St Lucia 78, 79
Steenbras Dam 147
Stellenbosch 149, 150
Storms River 104
Strand 145

Sun City 1, 39
Swartberg Pass 117
Swartkops River Mouth 102

Taalmonument 149
Thaba N'chu 39
Tongaat 81
Transkei 90-95
Tsitsikamma 105
Tulbagh 152

Umdloti 83
Umhlanga Rocks 83
Union Buildings 31
University of Cape Town 136
Upington 120

Valley of 1 000 Hills 71
Victoria and Alfred
    Waterfront 134
Victoria Embankment 63, 64-65
Village Walk, Sandton 16

Waenhuiskrans 158
Welkom 52, 53
Winburg 55
Worcester 152

The lighthouse at Cape Agulhas (*left*), southernmost point on the continent of Africa. The land here is relatively flat, part of an inland plain that slips under the sea to become the vast, shallow Agulhas Bank. The waters here are warmed by the southward-flowing Mocambique-Agulhas current, and the bank is regarded as one of the world's most bountiful fishing grounds.